A LITTLE COMMON SENSE™

Most mammals are wary of humans and are difficult to observe in the field. However, their presence can be detected by the signs (clues) they leave behind as they move from place to place. Signs include any disturbance or change to a natural environment, ranging from a blade of nibbled grass, to a track in the mud, to a hole in the ground. Knowing what to look for and how to differentiate signs makes detection relatively simple.

Key Signs

The key signs to look for include tracks and trails, droppings, feeding signs and nesting sites.

When to Look for Signs

The best times of the day for tracking are at dawn and dusk when most animals are leaving or returning to their home base. The best times of the year are in spring and early summer when many species are active throughout the day.

How to Track

1. Walk into the wind. Mammals have an excellent sense of smell and will leave an area once they pick up your scent.
2. Move slowly. Use binoculars to try to detect movement in the distance.
3. Be very quiet as you move. Move forward a few steps at a time and avoid stepping on twigs. Listen carefully for animals calling to each other or moving through the area.
4. Keep your distance. Move away from an animal if it stops feeding or appears nervous or startled.

Wildlife Watching Etiquette

1. Honor the rights of private landowners and other wildlife viewers.
2. Leave pets at home.
3. Large animals like elk, deer, moose, bighorn sheep, mountain lions and bears are dangerous. Use extreme caution to avoid attracting their attention.
4. Never touch orphaned or sick animals or try to feed wildlife; they can transmit deadly diseases like Hanta Virus via contact or by inhaling the virus. Contact your state wildlife agency if you find an animal injured or in distress.

Most illustrations show the adult male in breeding coloration. Colors and markings may be duller or absent during different seasons. The measurements denote the approximate maximum length of animals from nose to tail tip. Illustrations are not to scale.

Made in the USA

Waterford Press publishes reference guides that introduce readers to nature observation, outdoor recreation and survival skills. Product information is featured on the website: **www.waterfordpress.com**

Text & illustrations © 2010, 2022 Waterford Press Inc. All rights reserved. Photos © iStock Photo. To order or for information on custom published products please call 800-434-2555 or email orderdesk@waterfordpress.com. For permissions or to share comments email editor@waterfordpress.com.

ISBN 978-1-58355-551-4
$7.95 U.S.
50795
9 781583 555514
UPC 8 84682 00914 4
10 9 8 7 6 5 4 3 2 1
2206801

ANIMAL TRACKING – A Waterproof Folding Guide to Animal Tracking & Behavior

Kavanagh/Leung

A POCKET NATURALIST® GUIDE

ANIMAL TRACKING

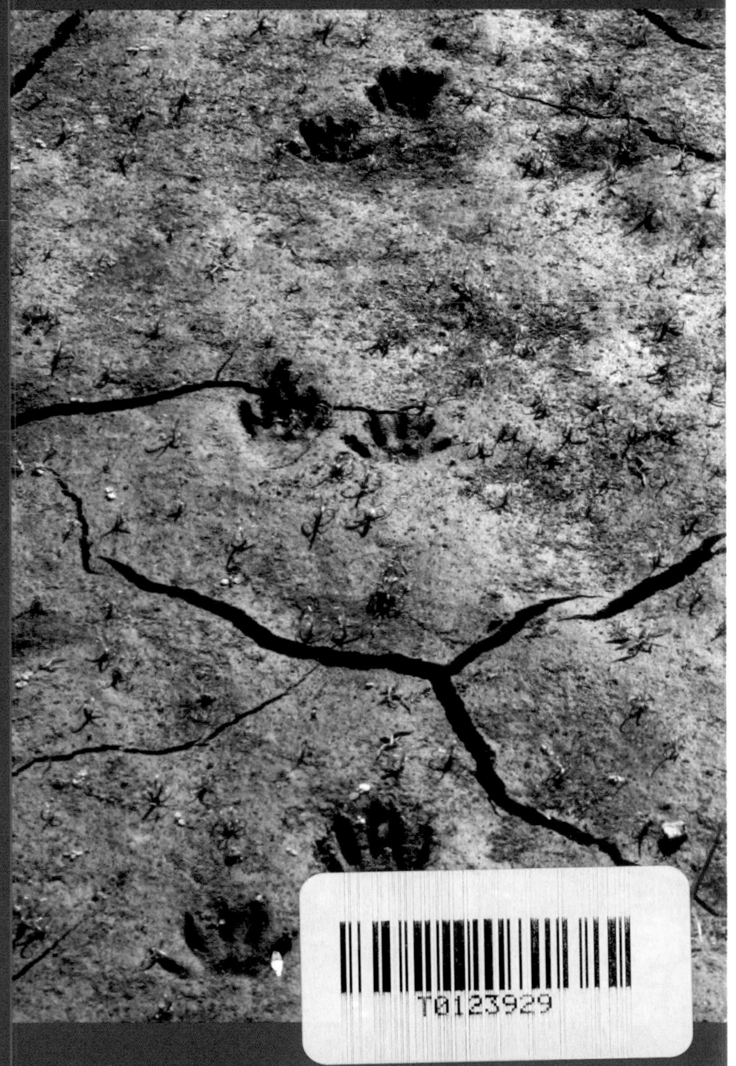

T0123929

A Waterproof Folding Guide to Animal Tracking & Behavior

DROPPINGS

The size, shape, color and content of droppings (scat) give key information about the animal and its diet. In general, the scats of predators are long and twisted and contain the fur, feathers or bones of its prey. Herbivores have 'pellet-like' or 'pie-like' scat depending on their diet and the time of year.

Rabbits & Hares
Distinctive round scats are about .5 in. (1.3 cm) long.

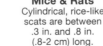

Squirrel
Cylindrical pellets are about .5 in. (1.3 cm) long.

Mice & Rats
Cylindrical, rice-like scats are between .3 in. and .8 in. (.8-2 cm) long.

Dog Family
Scat is usually a single cord with a pointed end. Droppings vary greatly in size and diameter and may be up to 5 in. (13 cm) long.

Porcupine
Pellets are about 1 in. (3 cm) long and often collect in huge piles in and around their dens and under trees.

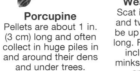

Weasel Family
Scat is usually black and twisted and may be up to 4 in. (10 cm) long. Family members include weasels, minks, skunks, otters and badgers.

Cat Family
Scat is usually segmented and often buried. It varies in size and may be up to 4 in. (10 cm) long.

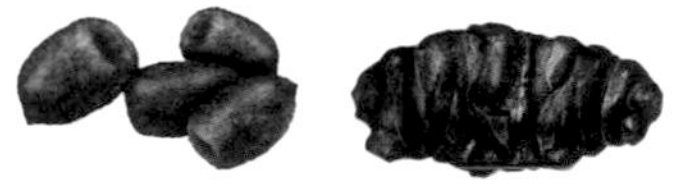

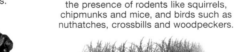

Deer Family
Distinctive pellet scats are pointed on one end and concave on the other. Scats vary in shape, but are about 1 in. (3 cm) long and deposited in small piles. Droppings are typically pellets in winter and chips or 'pies' in summer. Family members include deer, pronghorns, elk, mountain goats, caribou and bighorn sheep.

Northern River Otter
Scats are up to 7 in. (18 cm) long and .75 in. (2 cm) in diameter. Black when fresh, they are often deposited in piles in conspicuous places along the water's edge.

Moose
Oblong scats are about 1.5 in. (4 cm) long and deposited in large piles. Droppings in summer are loose 'pies'.

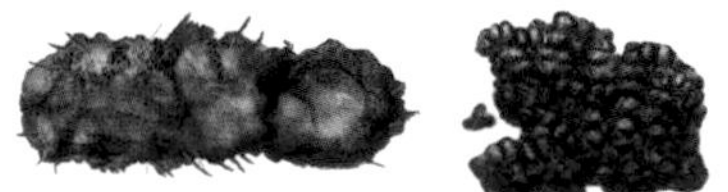

Bears
Scats are typically thick (to 2 in./5 cm wide) and cord-like, with blunt ends. When bears eat primarily vegetation, e.g., during the autumn berry season, scats form a loose mass, like a cow patty.

TIP If you find scat with berries or a distinguishable food source in it, locate the food source to find additional animal signs.

FEEDING SIGNS

Look for teeth marks on plants, nuts and bones. Bears will often tear up the earth in search of insects or rodents. Owls cough up fuzzy pellets of the fur and bones of rodents.

Browse
The browsed ends of twigs can indicate who ate them. Rabbits slice off the ends of twigs cleanly at a 45-degree angle. Porcupines leave rows of small bite marks on twig ends. Deer and moose break the ends off twigs and cause the tips to fray. Cats and dogs raggedly chew off the tops of grasses.

Gnawed Trees
Beaver sign.

Chewed Plants
Rodent or deer sign.

Chewed Nuts and Stripped Cones
Hollowed nuts and stripped cones indicate the presence of rodents like squirrels, chipmunks and mice, and birds such as nuthatches, crossbills and woodpeckers.

Squirrel Midden
A large pile of cone, nut and plant litter found beneath a favorite feeding spot, often at the base of a tree.

Beaver Sign
Beavers will stack branches in shallow water when preparing their food supply for winter.

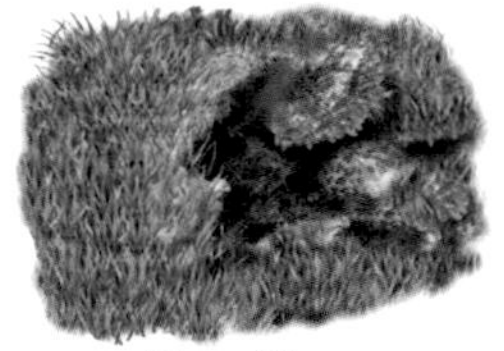

Bear Sign
Bears tear up large patches of earth while digging up roots and rodents.

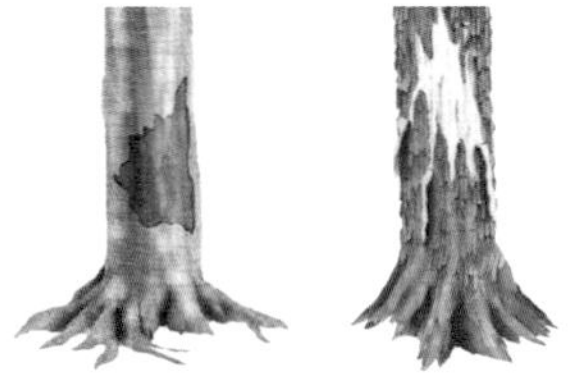

Barked Trees
Porcupines, beavers and hoofed mammals will chew off large patches of tree bark. Bears often tear the bark off the lower trunk to feed on sap.

Gnawed Bones
Mice, squirrels and other rodents leave teeth marks on the bones of dead animals.

Food Cache
Squirrels, chipmunks and mice often cache food in protected areas for the winter.

NESTING SITES

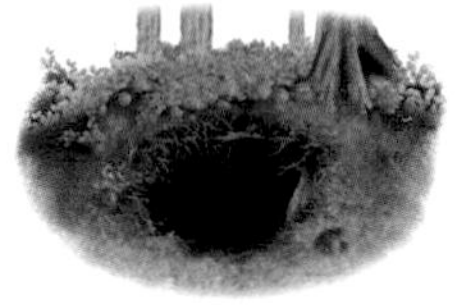

Den
Dens are protected areas excavated in vegetation, soil or under fallen logs by animals including rodents, foxes and bears. There is often a pile of scat near the entrance.

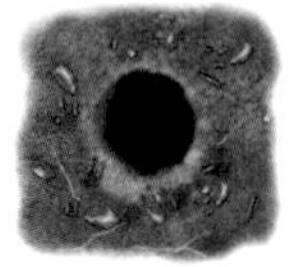

Burrow
A wide range of rodents from ground squirrels, badgers and woodchucks live in underground dens. There is usually a mound of dirt at the entrance to the burrow. The size of a tunnel indicates the size of the animal.

Squirrel Nest
Rounded nests of leaves and twigs are often located in a crotch of tree branches.

Mouse Nest
Rounded nests are made of grasses and are often located above the ground in the branches of shrubs.

Tree Hole
Usually drilled by woodpeckers, they can be home to a variety of creatures.

Rabbit Nest
Rabbits create slight depressions in the earth and use grasses and their fur to line the nest and create a lid to cover it.

Beaver Lodge
Lodge is located in the middle of a pond and is constructed primarily of sticks and mud. Size is variable, but is typically over 4 ft. (1.2 m) high and 10 ft. (3 m) in diameter.

Muskrat Lodge
Dome-shaped lodge is constructed of marsh plants and mud. Size is variable, but they are typically over 2 ft. (60 cm) high and 3 ft. (90 cm) in diameter.

OTHER SIGNS

Smells
Many animals like skunks, weasels and foxes have distinctive smells. Bears smell like rotting garbage. Wolves, deer and mountain lions often mark their territory by depositing scat or spraying fetid urine on objects.

Sounds
Wolves and coyotes howl, elk bugle, rabbits and hares thump their back feet on the ground when they sense danger, beavers slap their tails on the water before diving for the same reason. Marmots and prairie dogs whistle loudly when danger approaches.

OTHER SIGNS

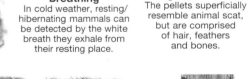

Bedding Areas
Deer and other hoofed mammals create oval areas of matted vegetation where they sleep.

Trails
Many animals establish well-worn trails between their home base and feeding/watering areas. Deer, for example, create distinct well-worn trails through forests and fields that can be generations old. Many small rodents create hidden 'runways' in dense grass and snow.

Scratch Marks on Trees
Bears will claw and bite trees as high as they can reach. Bobcats sometimes use trees as 'scratching posts'. Rodents and raccoons leave scratch marks on trees while climbing. Male deer will often rub the bark off the lower extremities of smaller trees with their antlers.

Bird Pellet
Owls, eagles, hawks, ravens and gulls are a few species of birds that commonly regurgitate pellets comprised of undigestible material. The pellets superficially resemble animal scat, but are comprised of hair, feathers and bones.

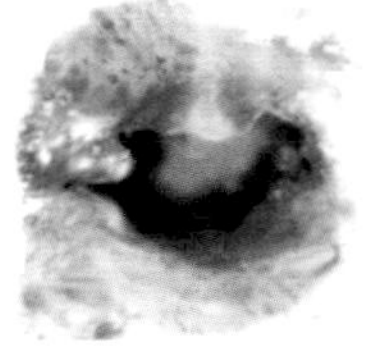

Breathing
In cold weather, resting/hibernating mammals can be detected by the white breath they exhale from their resting place.

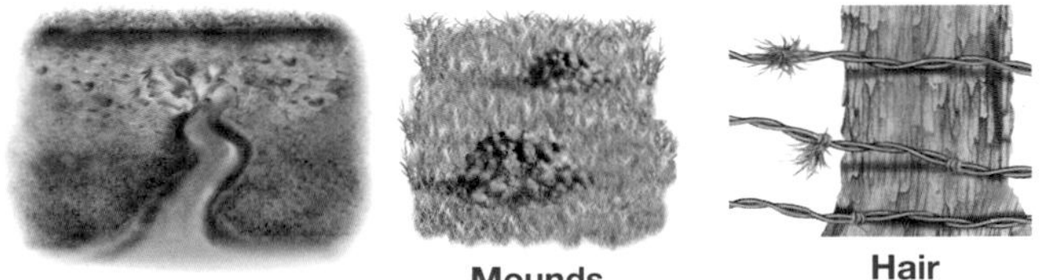

Slides
River otters often create 'slides' on the banks of ponds or rivers that they use when entering the water.

Mounds
Moles and pocket gophers rarely surface but their presence can be detected by the mounds of earth they push up while tunneling.

Hair
When animals brush against fences, trees or logs, they often leave behind tufts of hair. Look for tracks in the area to decipher who the hair belongs to.

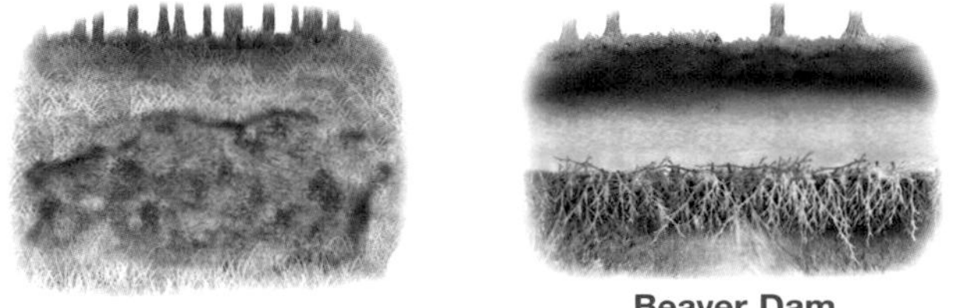

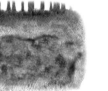

Scraped Depression/Wallow
During mating season, male elk, deer and moose will paw the vegetation off an area of earth and mark the site with urine or feces.

Beaver Dam
Beavers create a linear pile of logs at right angles to the water flow in order to create a pond in which to build their lodge. They can be several feet high and up to 100 yds. (91 m) long.

One of the easiest signs to interpret, an animal's track is defined by the shape of its feet, its weight, and the way it walks, runs or hops. The size of a track generally indicates the size of the animal. Sandy or muddy soils are the best places to find clear tracks. The best time to look for tracks is following rains, fresh snowfalls, or at dawn when the dew makes tracks easy to identify.

While measurements given are of maximum sizes, they are intended to serve as general guidelines; keep in mind that tracks are influenced by several factors including the age and size of the animal, the material it walks on, the season (some mammals grow extra fur between their toes in winter), the age of the track and the animal's stride (is it walking, loping or running?).

The pattern of tracks is also a good indicator of the species. Generally speaking, there are four kinds of track patterns. Deer, dog and cats are **diagonal walkers** and walk with a front foot and the opposite back foot moving at the same time. Most weasels are **bounders** and push off with their front feet, have their back feet land near the front feet tracks, and then push off with the back feet. Rabbits and most rodents are **gallopers** that push off with their back feet and land on their front feet with the front tracks behind the rear tracks. Lastly, raccoons, bears, porcupines and beavers are **amblers** which move with a front foot and same side back foot moving at the same time.

Dogs

Dog tracks show claws. The foot pad is small in relation to the toes and has a single lobe. They range in size from 2 in./5 cm long (kit fox) to 5 in./13 cm long (gray wolf). Wolves and coyotes are very vocal and make a variety of calls and choruses.

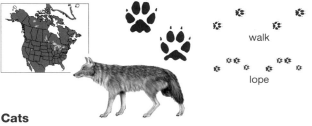

walk

lope

Cats

Cat tracks do not show claws. The foot pad is large in relation to the toes and has two lobes. Note the rounded toe pads. They range in size from 2 in./5 cm long (bobcat) to 4 in./10 cm long (mountain lion).

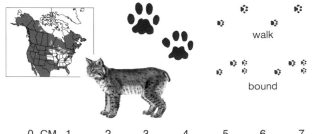

walk

bound

Rabbits & Hares

Rabbits and hares all have rear feet at least twice as long as their front feet. When they bound, they land with their hind feet in front of their forefeet. As they speed up, their hind feet land further in front of their forefeet.

hop

jackrabbit gallop

Bear

Bear tracks show claws. Human-like hind print ranges in size from 6 in./15 cm long (black bear) to 12 in./30 cm long (grizzly). Track is pigeon-toed. When the animal is ambling (a fast walk) the hind foot overtakes the front foot.

amble

gallop

Raccoon

Tracks are like small hands. Hind prints are 4 in. (10 cm) long and claws are clearly visible. Hips roll while walking causing the hind foot to register beside the opposite front foot.

walk

gallop

Opossum

Distinctive, hand-like tracks are about 2 in. (5 cm) wide. Tracks show tail dragging on ground between feet.

Badger

Tracks are 2-3 in. (5-8 cm) long. Claw marks are longer on the fore print. Key signs are dens with large oval openings.

walk   walk

Skunk

Hind print is 2-3 in. (5-8 cm) long; fore print is 1-2 in. (3-5 cm) long. Claws are often only evident on fore prints. Rotten egg smell is a key sign.

overstep walk

Common Muskrat

Hind track is about 3 in. (8 cm) long and has 5 toes. Leaves scat in piles near waterline. Look for floating grassy lodges near shore.

walk

American Beaver

These animals have webbed feet. Hind tracks are about 6 in. (15 cm) long and the webbing between the toes is often visible in mud.

walk

Northern River Otter

The otter's spreading tracks are about 3 in. (8 cm) across and claws are visible. Webbing between the back toes is often evident in mud.

walk

Squirrels/Chipmunks

Hind tracks are 1-2 in. (3-5 cm) long with 5 toes. Front tracks are smaller and show 4 toes.

bound

Ground Squirrels

Hind tracks are 1-2 in. (3-5 cm) in length with 5 long toes.

bound

Prairie Dog

Hind tracks are about 1.5 in. (4 cm) long with 5 toes. Front tracks show 4 toes.

walk

Deer Mouse

Hind track is about .7 in. (1.8 cm) long. Front track shows 4 toes. Tracks in soft soil usually show tail drag between feet.

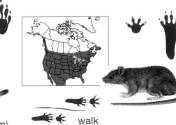

walk

Porcupine

Hind tracks are 3-4 in. (8-10 cm) long. Note straight toes. Claws are prominent. An ambler, it walks with its front foot and same side back foot moving at the same time. Leaves piles of droppings at tree base. Chews large patches of bark off trees. Smells like chicken soup.

walk

Norway Rat

Hind tracks show 5 toes and are 1.5-2.5 in. (4-6 cm) long. Front tracks show 4 toes and are about 1 in. (3 cm) long. Tracks in soft soil usually show tail drag between feet.

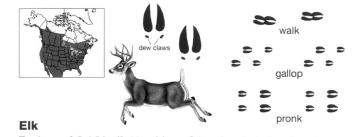

walk

Woodchuck/Groundhog

Hind tracks are about 2.5 in. (6 cm) long and have 5 toes. Front tracks show 4 toes. Look for tracks near burrow entrance.

walk

Armadillo

Distinctive tracks have 5 toes on the hind foot and 4 on the front foot and are 1-2 in. (3-5 cm) long. Claws are prominent. Tracks in soft soil usually show tail drag between feet.

walk

Deer

Tracks are 2-3 in. (5-8 cm) long. Dew claws are evident in soft soil, snow and when running. A 'pronk' is a trail left when the deer bounces forward with its front and rear hooves hitting the ground at the same time.

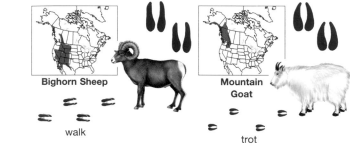

dew claws

walk

gallop

pronk

Elk

Tracks are 3.5-4.5 in. (9-11 cm) long. Other signs include antler rubs on small trees and wallows during mating season. Males are very vocal in the fall and 'bugle' loudly to challenge other males.

walk

gallop

Moose

Tracks are 5-6 in. (13-15 cm) long and more pointed than the elk's. Dew claws are often evident in soft soil, snow and when running.

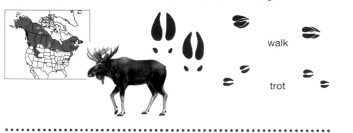

walk

trot

HOW TO CAST AN ANIMAL TRACK IN PLASTER

Plaster is available at most craft and hardware stores. You'll also need a container for mixing and some water.

1. Find a distinct track and remove any debris from the area.
2. Create a wall around the track by using a cardboard ring or build a dirt berm.
3. Mix plaster and pour onto the edge of the track until it rises up the sides of the wall.
4. Let plaster set for half an hour before removing cast.
5. Let cast set a day before cleaning it.

Pronghorn

Tracks are 2.5-3.5 in. (6-9 cm) long and wider at the base than those of deer. Dew claws are not evident.

amble

walk

gallop

Sheep & Goats

Bighorn sheep and mountain goats both have tracks that are 2.5-3.5 in. (6-9 cm) long. Hoof prints are splayed when running. Toes may be spread in front, making the tracks look square.

Bighorn Sheep

Mountain Goat

walk

trot

Peccary & Wild Boar

Native collared peccaries (javelinas) have rounded tracks that are 1-2 in. (3-5 cm) long and lack dew claws. The introduced wild boar has tracks 2-3 in. (5-8 cm) long and prominent dew claws. Both leave similar trail patterns.

Collared Peccary

Wild Boar

walk

trot

BUILD A TRACKING BOX

1. Build a box 6 ft. X 4 ft. X 6 in. deep (1.8 m X 1.2 m X 15 cm).
2. Place the box near a natural food or water source. Fill the box with sand or muddy soil that will yield clear tracks. Rake the soil smooth.
3. Study the box daily for fresh tracks. Re-rake as needed.

0 CM 1 2 3 4 5 6 7 8 9 10 11 12 13 14 15 16 17 18 19 20 21 22 23 24 25 26 27 28 29 30 31 32 33 34 35 36 37 38 39 40 41 42 43 44 45 46 47 48 49 50 51 52 53 54

0 INCHES 1 2 3 4 5 6 7 8 9 10 11 12 13 14 15 16 17 18 19 20 21